I LOVE MUSIC:

ALL ABOUT MUSICAL INSTRUMENTS THEN AND NOW

Speedy Publishing LLC
40 E. Main St. #1156
Newark, DE 19711
www.speedypublishing.com

Copyright 2015

All Rights reserved. No part of this book may be reproduced or used in any way or form or by any means whether electronic or mechanical, this means that you cannot record or photocopy any material ideas or tips that are provided in this book

A musical instrument is an instrument created or adapted to make musical sounds. The history of musical instruments dates to the beginnings of human culture.

MUSICAL INSTRUMENTS

THEN

Lute is a stringed musical instrument having a long, fretted neck and a hollow, typically pear-shaped body with a vaulted back. The player of a lute is called a lutenist and a maker of lutes is referred to as a luthier.

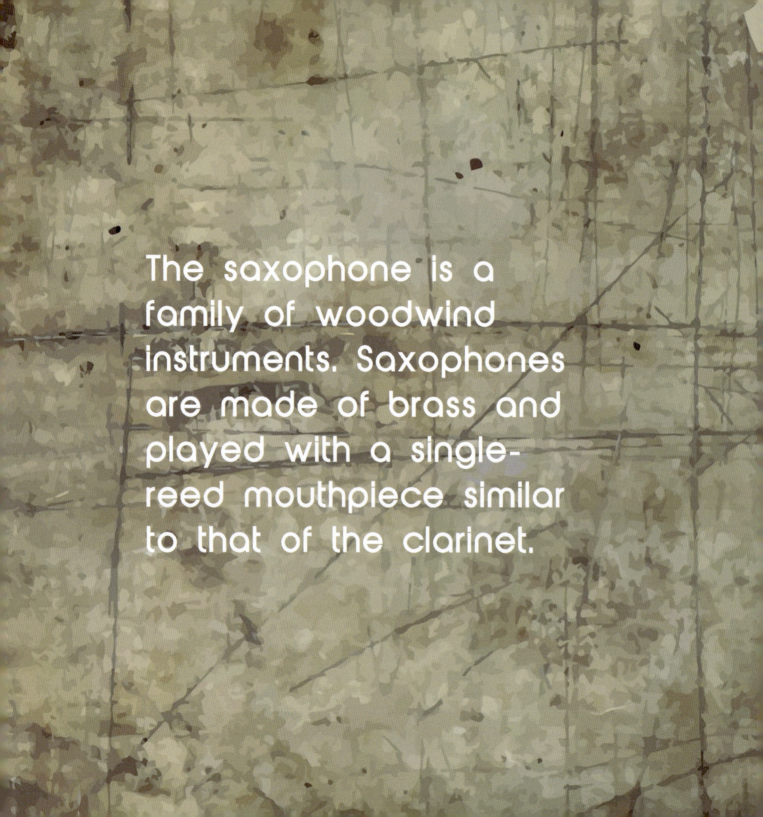

The saxophone is a family of woodwind instruments. Saxophones are made of brass and played with a single-reed mouthpiece similar to that of the clarinet.

The harp is a stringed musical instrument which has a number of individual strings running at an angle to its soundboard, which are plucked with the fingers. Harps are essentially triangular in shape, and are made primarily of wood.

The pipe organ is a musical instrument that produces sound by driving pressurized air through pipes. A pipe organ has one or more keyboards played by the hands, and a pedalboard played by the feet, each of which has its own group of stops.

Timpani are musical instruments in the percussion family. Timpani are struck with a special type of drum stick fittingly called a timpani stick.

Harmonica is a musical wind instrument consisting of a small rectangular case containing a set of metal reeds connected to a row of holes. Harmonica is played by using the mouth to direct air into and out of one or more holes along a mouthpiece.

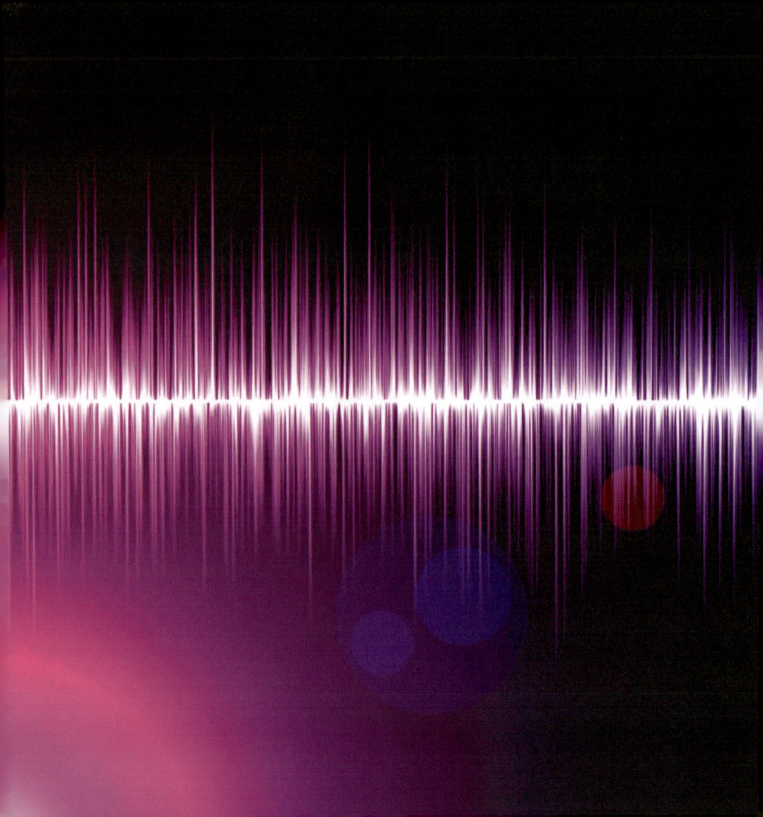

MUSICAL INSTRUMENTS

NOW

An electric guitar is a guitar equipped with electric or magnetic pickups that permit its sound to be amplified and fed to a loudspeaker.

A sound synthesizer s an electronic musical instrument that generates electric signals converted to sound through loudspeakers or headphones.

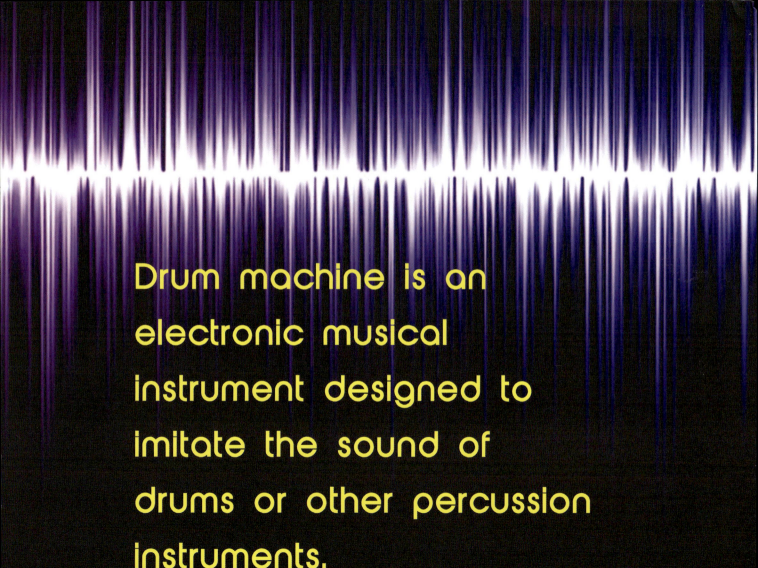

MIDI keyboard is typically a piano-style user interface keyboard device used for sending MIDI signals or commands over a USB or MIDI cable to other devices connected and operating on the same MIDI protocol interface.

An electronic drum is an electrical device struck by a drummer, played in real time to produce a selection of sounds.

A turntable is a musical device DJ's use to play records. Some turntablists use turntable techniques like beat mixing/matching, scratching, and beat juggling.

Printed in Great Britain
by Amazon